HISTORY'S GREATEST RIVALS

ROBERT PEARY

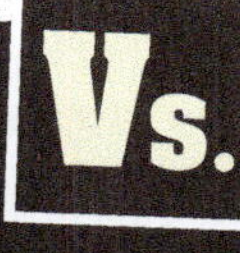

FREDERICK COOK

RACE TO THE NORTH POLE

Ellis Roxburgh

Please visit our website, **www.garethstevens.com**.
For a free color catalog of all our high-quality books,
call toll-free 1-800-542-2595 or fax 1-877-542-2596.

Cataloging-in-Publication Data

Roxburgh, Ellis.
Robert Peary vs. Frederick Cook: Race to the North Pole / by Ellis Roxburgh.
p. cm. — (History's greatest rivals)
Includes index.
ISBN 978-1-4824-4231-1 (pbk.)
ISBN 978-1-4824-4232-8 (6-pack)
ISBN 978-1-4824-4233-5 (library binding)
1. Peary, Robert E. — (Robert Edwin), — 1856-1920 — Juvenile literature. 2. Cook, Frederick Albert, — 1865-1940. 3. Explorers — United States — Biography — Juvenile literature. 4. North Pole — Discovery and exploration — Juvenile literature. I. Roxburgh, Ellis. II. Title.
G635.P4 R69 2016
910'.9163'2—d23

Published in 2016 by
Gareth Stevens Publishing
111 East 14th Street, Suite 349
New York, NY 10003

For Brown Bear Books Ltd:
Editorial Director: Lindsey Lowe
Managing Editor: Tim Cooke
Children's Publisher: Anne O'Daly
Design Manager: Keith Davis
Designer: Lynne Lennon
Picture Manager: Sophie Mortimer

Picture Credits: T=Top, C=Center, B=Bottom, L=Left, R=Right. Front Cover: Library of Congress: l; Robert Hunt Library: r; Shutterstock: Volodymyr Goinyk background. Dreamstime: 34, Andre & Anita 20, Eli Mitchell 13; Esmée la Fleur: 33; Library of Congress: 10, 11, 12, 15, 18, 19, 21, 22, 25, 26, 30, 39; Mary Evans Picture Library: 36; NARA: 23, 32; National Geographic Creative: Sisse Brimberg 35; National Geographic Society: 29; Robert Hunt Library: 6, 8, 14, 16, 17, 27; RTE, History Canada: 7; Shutterstock: Zack Frank 37; Christopher Wood 40; Thinkstock: Cory Glencross 9, Photos.com 31; Topfoto: 24, 28, ullsteinbild 38; WallyHerbert.com 41.

Manufactured in the United States of America

CPSIA compliance information: Batch #CW16GS. For further information contact Gareth Stevens, New York, New York at 1-800-542-2595.

CONTENTS

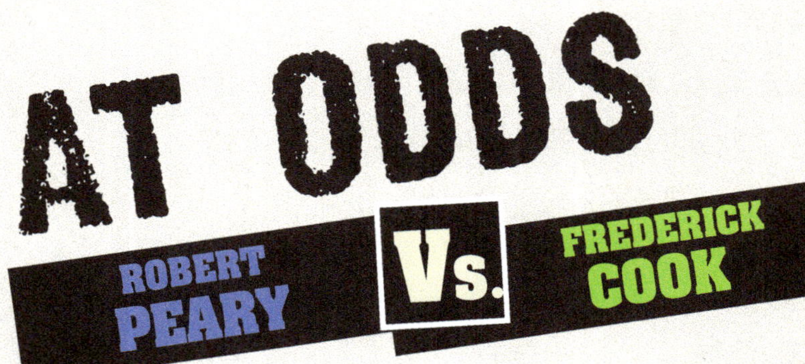

Robert Peary (1856–1920) was determined to become an American hero. From a young age, he was fascinated by polar exploration.

* Peary trained as a civil engineer in the US Navy. In 1885 he had decided to be the first man to reach the North Pole.
* Peary had no interest in advancing scientific knowledge about the Arctic region, only in reaching his goal.
* He attracted many wealthy backers for his six trips to the Arctic.
* Peary led large, well-publicized expeditions to the Arctic.

Dr. Frederick Cook (1865–1940) was an explorer who was fascinated by the world's most remote places and the indigenous peoples who lived there.

* **Cook trained as a doctor. His medical knowledge was invaluable on his many expeditions.**

* **Cook wanted to further scientific advances on his journeys.**

* **He did not have organized financial backing and paid for his expeditions from his physician's salary and his savings.**

* **Cook was introspective and self-sufficient. He traveled with few people on his expeditions and relied on the expertise of local peoples.**

CONTEXT

Until late in the 19th century, explorers had not tried to reach the North Pole. Instead they explored the Arctic in the hopes of finding a sea route to Asia.

From the 16th century onward Arctic explorers had tried to find the Northwest Passage. This was a much talked about sea route around the top of North America to Asia. If it existed, it would provide a way for Europeans to trade with East Asia without having to rely on the goodwill of peoples who controlled the land routes through Asia. British explorers dominated early attempts to find the Northwest Passage. Between 1776 and 1779, the famous British navigator Captain James Cook sailed north up the American west coast as far as the Bering Strait in the hope of finding it. He failed. Any possible route lay within the Arctic Circle, and this was almost permanently blocked by ice.

CONTACT: The Scottish explorer John Ross meets Inuit in Greenland on his expedition to search for the Northwest Passage in 1818.

STUCK: This drawing shows the ships of Sir John Franklin's expedition frozen in the Arctic ice.

In 1819 a British naval officer named William Edward Parry (1790–1855) became the first person to reach the Arctic Archipelago, a group of islands that lie north of Canada, before solid ice blocked his way.

> "The lure of the North! It is a strange and powerful thing."

Robert Peary in *Nearest the Pole* (1907)

A Doomed Expedition

In 1845, Sir John Franklin (1786-1847) set out with two ships and 129 men in search of the Northwest Passage. None of them returned. A number of land and sea expeditions were later launched to try to solve the mystery of what had happened to Franklin and his crew aboard their ships *Erebus* and the *Terror*. After some of their possessions were discovered with local Inuit in 1853, it was confirmed that everyone on the expedition had died. After that time, British interest in Arctic exploration faded.

In 1878, the Finnish-born Swede Baron Adolf Erik Nordenskiöld (1832-1901) became the first person to successfully navigate the Northeast Passage. This was a sea route to Asia around the top of what is now Russia. Nordenskiöld's success encouraged US explorers to start their own investigation of the little-known Arctic region.

TRAGEDY: Adolphus Greely's expedition was stuck in the Arctic for three years and 18 men died.

A New Goal

As more explorers headed to the Arctic, they began competing to get as far north as possible. In 1882, Adolphus Greely (1844–1935) led a US expedition to set up an observation base in the Arctic. During the expedition, Lieutenant James B. Lockwood (1852–1884) got farther north than anyone had gone before. Greely's expedition ended in tragedy when 18 men, including Lockwood, died of starvation, drowning, or cold; only six men

OCEAN: Early explorers believed the Arctic was a frozen continent. In fact, it was a frozen sea.

survived. Despite its tragic end, Lockwood's achievement sparked more interest in the idea of reaching the North Pole.

As early as 1885, when no one else was really thinking about reaching the North Pole, Robert Peary wrote in his diary that he intended to be the first man to get there. He later planned and carried out seven expeditions to try to achieve his ambition. However, the efforts to find the Northwest Passage had been made by ship. To reach the North Pole, explorers would have to walk across the frozen Arctic Ocean, relying on sleds and skis to help them.

> "We are at the top of the world!"
>
> **Frederick Cook, diary entry, April 21, 1908**

ROBERT PEARY

» A SINGLE-MINDED PURSUIT

Peary decided early in his career that he would dedicate his life to becoming the first man to reach the North Pole.

FURS: The Inuit taught Peary to wear furs for warmth. Other explorers continued to wear canvas clothes.

Robert Edwin Peary was born in Pennsylvania in 1856. After his father died in 1859, he and his mother moved to Maine. Peary was close to his mother. She later lived with Peary and his wife, Josephine.

In 1881, Peary joined the US Navy Civil Engineers Corps. Three years later the Navy sent him to Nicaragua on a canal surveying project. The trip had a huge influence on the rest of Peary's life. On the expedition, he met Matthew Henson (1866–1955), who would become his assistant. It was also while in Nicaragua that Peary decided to make a career of Arctic exploration.

Influential Friends

Peary wrote in his diary that he was determined to be the first man to the North Pole. In 1886 his mother funded his first expedition to

PROJECT: This is the US Navy camp where Peary worked as a surveyor in Nicaragua in 1881.

Greenland. When he returned to Greenland again in 1891, the expedition doctor was Peary's later rival, Frederick Cook. Peary's later expeditions were funded by the Peary Arctic Club. These influential supporters paid for the latest state-of-the-art equipment. On his seventh expedition in 1909 Peary claimed to have reached the North Pole. In recognition of his achievement he received many honors and was made an admiral. He died in 1920. Cook had warned him years earlier that spending time in the harsh conditions of the Arctic would damage his health. This turned out to be the case.

> "Peary is wrecked in ambition, wrecked in physique, and wrecked in hope."

Cook reports to the Peary Arctic Club, Summer 1901

FREDERICK COOK

» A CURIOUS DOCTOR

Frederick Cook had a great interest in different cultures around the world. However, his career as an explorer began with a personal tragedy.

Frederick Albert Cook was born into a family that had emigrated from Germany and changed their name from Koch to Cook. He was born in upstate New York in 1865. He studied medicine at Columbia University. While Cook was waiting for the results of his final examinations in 1891, his young wife died in childbirth. He did not remarry until 1902. Cook joined Robert Peary's Greenland expedition as doctor in 1891. The trip gave him a lifelong interest in other cultures and remote places.

DOCTOR: Cook's medical skill saved many members of polar expeditions who fell sick.

Other Expeditions

From 1897 to 1899, Cook traveled to the Antarctic on the Belgian Antarctic Expedition. In 1897 he visited Tierra del Fuego at the tip of South America. In 1903, Cook led an expedition to

PEAK: In 1906 Cook claimed to be the first man to reach the top of Mount McKinley.

Alaska's Mount McKinley. Cook visited the mountain again in 1906, when he claimed to have reached its summit.

In his later life, Cook moved to Texas and worked in the oil business. In 1923, he was sent to jail for fraud but was released in 1930. President Franklin D. Roosevelt pardoned him in 1940, shortly before Cook's death.

> "In Dr. Cook we have one of the few Americans, if not the only American, who has explored both extremes of the world, the Arctic and the Antarctic regions."

Alexander Graham Bell, December 15, 1906, addressing National Geographic dinner in honor of Peary.

PEARY'S CLUB

» POWERFUL SUPPORTERS

Robert Peary had some powerful friends. He also had the support of the wealthy backers who formed the Peary Arctic Club.

BABY: Josephine Peary wrote this book about the birth of her daughter, Marie Ahnighito.

Peary formed the Peary Arctic Club in 1898. Its members were friends of Peary with money and influence. They included Morris K. Jesup, a banker and philanthropist who since 1881 was president of the American Museum of Natural History. Members of the Peary Arctic Club introduced Peary to other backers such as President Theodore Roosevelt. Peary named his ship *Roosevelt* for the US president, who saw him off when he left for the Arctic.

Two individuals showed lasting loyalty to Peary: his wife, Josephine Diebitsch Peary (1863–1955), and his assistant, Matthew Henson. Josephine accompanied Peary on some of his Arctic expeditions. She published her observations of life in the polar regions as *My Arctic*

PIONEER: Matthew Henson was the first African American Arctic explorer.

Journal (1893). She even gave birth to their daughter, Marie Ahnighito, in the Arctic in 1893. In 1900 Josephine and Marie went to visit Peary, who was then in northern Greenland. When their ship was damaged, they had to spend the whole winter in the Arctic.

> **"I believe in you, Peary, and I believe in your success, if it is within the possibility of man!"**
>
> **President Theodore Roosevelt, July 7, 1908**

Peary met Henson, an African American, in Nicaragua in 1881. They made six expeditions together. Peary asked Henson to make the trip to the North Pole in 1909. Henson's diary later helped explorers conclude that Peary had not reached the Pole after all.

COOK'S FRIENDS

» THE EXPLORER'S EXPLORER

Frederick Cook lacked Peary's influential supporters, but he did inspire great loyalty among fellow explorers and adventurers.

MASTER: Roald Amundsen held many "firsts" of polar exploration.

One of Cook's lifelong friends was the most famous of all polar explorers. Cook met the Norwegian Roald Amundsen (1872–1928) on the 1897–1899 Belgian Antarctic Expedition. In 1903–1906 Amundsen became the first man to sail through the Northwest Passage and in 1911 he was the first man to reach the South Pole. In 1926 he reached the North Pole by airship. When the National Geographic Society invited Amundsen to the United States to give a talk, Amundsen went to visit Cook, who was then in jail in Kansas. The National Geographic Society was a supporter of Peary. It was angry that Amundsen had visited Cook and withdrew its invitation.

Harry Whitney

Another friend who had a huge influence on Cook's life was the millionaire Harry Whitney (1873–1936). Whitney sailed on board Peary's *Roosevelt* in 1908 and met Cook on his return from the North

CAPT. BARTLETT AND HARRY WHITNEY TO LEAD AMERICAN EXPEDITION TO SEEK SOUTH POLE

First Announcement Through The Times of an American Effort to Plant the Stars and Stripes in the Furthest Antarctic by Peary's Old Captain and the Well-Known Arctic Traveler — A Race Against Scott's English Expedition.

TREK: In 1910 Harry Whitney announced a plan to reach the South Pole, but the trip never took place.

Pole in April 1909. Cook asked Whitney to look after his equipment while Cook rushed home. Whitney himself got a ride home with Peary, but Peary refused to carry Cook's equipment. Without his equipment, Cook could not prove he had reached the North Pole.

For his expedition to the Pole, Cook relied on the Inuit. He made the final part of his trek with two Inuit, named Etukishook and Ahwelah. According to Whitney, they were skilled sled handlers who helped Cook travel faster over the ice toward the pole.

> **"The Dr. Cook I knew as a young man (was) the soul of honor and kindliness, lion-hearted in courage."**
>
> **Amundsen on his visit to Cook in prison, January 1926**

LINES ARE DRAWN

» EARLY EXPLORATIONS AND DISPUTES

In 1891, Robert Peary set off on his second expedition to Greenland. Among his crew was the ship's doctor, Frederick Cook.

GIFTS: On board ship, Peary hands out presents to Inuit from Greenland.

On his first expedition in 1886, Peary had attempted to cross Greenland by dog sled. He traveled nearly 100 miles (160 km) across the ice sheet before a lack of food forced him to turn back.

Peary set off again in 1891. He wanted to find out if Greenland was an island or if it was joined to the North Pole. Peary broke his leg badly during the voyage to Greenland. Cook set his bones. After his leg healed, Peary set out across Greenland. When he saw the distant sea he concluded Greenland was an island.

BASE: Peary built a hut in Greenland in 1891 to store the expedition supplies.

A Falling Out

Peary returned to the Arctic in 1893. He asked the members of the expedition to agree not to publish anything about the new journey before he had done so. Cook would not agree. The two men fell out and Cook quit the new expedition. Cook and Peary met again in 1901. Peary had gone missing in the Arctic, and his family asked Cook to find him. Cook found Peary. He may have saved Peary's life by treating him for scurvy and heart problems.

> "I pulled this thing off finally, and then to have the whole matter soiled and smirched by a cowardly dog of an imposter."

Peary writing about Cook's claim to have reached the Pole, July 22, 1910

RIVAL JOURNEYS

FLASH POINT » TWO CLAIMS TO REACH THE POLE

By around 1907 Cook and Peary were both ready to try to be the first to reach the North Pole. Cook set off first, without much publicity.

In July 1907, Frederick Cook sailed out of New York on a sailing ship named *John R. Bradley*. The ship belonged to a wealthy sportsman of the same name. John R. Bradley was a member of the Explorers Club, which had been set up in 1905 to encourage exploration. When he set out, Cook only said he was going hunting. He only announced his plan to reach the North Pole when he was already in the Arctic.

ICESCAPE: Cook later described the Arctic as a frozen ocean with huge barriers of ice.

FLAG: Two of Cook's party pose with the American flag at the North Pole.

Cook's Attempt

Cook spent the winter of 1907 in the small settlement of Annoatok in Greenland, some 700 miles (1,126 km) from the North Pole. In February 1908, he set out with nine Inuit, 11 sleds, and 103 dogs. He followed a route that had previously been mapped by a Norwegian expedition. When he was within 360 miles (580 km) of the pole, Cook took his two most trusted Inuit, Etukishook and Ahwelah, to make the final part of the journey. In 24 days the three

> "What a cheerless spot to have aroused the ambition of man for so many ages!"

Frederick Cook, September 1, 1909

> "The Pole at last!!! The prize of three centuries, my dream and ambition for twenty-three years. Mine at last."

Robert Peary's diary entry for April 9, 1909

men covered an average of 15 miles (24 km) a day. They reached the North Pole on April 21, 1908. Cook claimed to have buried a note in a brass tube in a crevasse at the Pole as a record of his achievement.

FLAGS: Peary's expedition displays flags at the North Pole, including the flags of the United States and the Navy League.

The three men then turned back. The return journey was disastrous. The pack ice had melted and their way was blocked by open water. They were stuck in the Arctic Archipelago over the winter. It took almost a year to return to Greenland, and they almost starved to death on the way.

Peary's Journey

Meanwhile, Peary had left New York about a year after Cook, in July 1908. He traveled on the ship *Roosevelt*. The ship could cut through pack ice with ease. Peary and his expedition arrived at Cape Sheridan on Ellesmere Island later in the summer. He spent the winter there and set off for the North Pole on March 1, 1909. Peary's starting point was hundreds of miles closer to the North Pole than Cook had been. Peary left Ellesmere Island with 24 men, 19 sleds, and 133 dogs. He used what he called the "Peary System," which he developed in 1906. It used sleds pulled by dogs to send supplies ahead of the explorers.

At the end of March Peary's support group turned back. Peary, Matthew Henson, four Inuit, and 40 dogs made the final march to the pole. According to Peary's later accounts, they reached the North Pole on April 6, 1909. Peary and his companions spent 30 hours at the pole before turning back for home.

HERO: Matthew Henson became celebrated as a pioneer of African American exploration, as in this later textbook.

GETTING HOME

FLASH POINT » HITCHING A RIDE WITH PEARY

Cook and Peary were shocked to discover each other's claims to have reached the North Pole. They both raced for home to tell their stories first.

Cook finally returned to Annoatok in Greenland in April 1909, 14 months after he had left on his way to the North Pole. In Annoatok he met the American sportsman Harry Whitney, who told him that Peary had set out on March 1, 1909, to attempt to reach the North Pole. Whitney also told him most people believed Cook was dead. Cook was anxious to return to his family. The first available ship was a whaler sailing to Denmark, but it had no room for his equipment, such as his sextant. Cook left his belongings with Whitney, who promised to take them back when he later returned to the United States.

LECTURE: Cook describes his expedition to an audience in Copenhagen, Denmark.

Peary Appears

After Cook left, the ship Whitney had hired to take him home failed to turn up. In August 1909 Peary offered Whitney a ride on the *Roosevelt*. Peary was returning from

***ROOSEVELT*: Peary refused to allow Cook's possessions on board his ship.**

his own trip to the North Pole. While in Annoatok, Peary heard the news that Cook had made it to the Pole before him. It was only then Peary mentioned that he had himself reached the North Pole. Peary refused to let Whitney take Cook's possessions on board. Whitney buried them in an underground cache. Cook said later that when he had received the news from Whitney, he felt "sick." He had no evidence to prove he had ever made it to the North Pole.

> **"Peary would allow nothing belonging to you onboard. Said leave everything in cache."**
>
> **Harry Whitney, telegram to Cook, end of September 1909**

RIVAL CLAIMS

FLASH POINT » **CONTRADICTORY ACCOUNTS**

Men had tried to reach the North Pole for 300 years. Now Cook and Peary both claimed within five days of each other to have reached it.

RECEPTION: Cook (center) receives a hero's welcome in New York on August 21, 1909.

Cook reached New York from Denmark on August 21, 1909. Some 100,000 New Yorkers lined the streets to give him a hero's welcome. Cook was interviewed first in Copenhagen, Denmark, and again in the United States. He was modest about his achievement.

According to newspapers at the time, most people saw no reason to doubt Cook's account. He had his notebook recording his journey, and explained that his sextant and other equipment were on their way back from Greenland. Only later did Cook learn that Harry Whitney had left them behind. Meanwhile, Robert Peary arrived back in the United States. He did not talk much about his own journey to the Pole. Instead, he set out to discredit Cook.

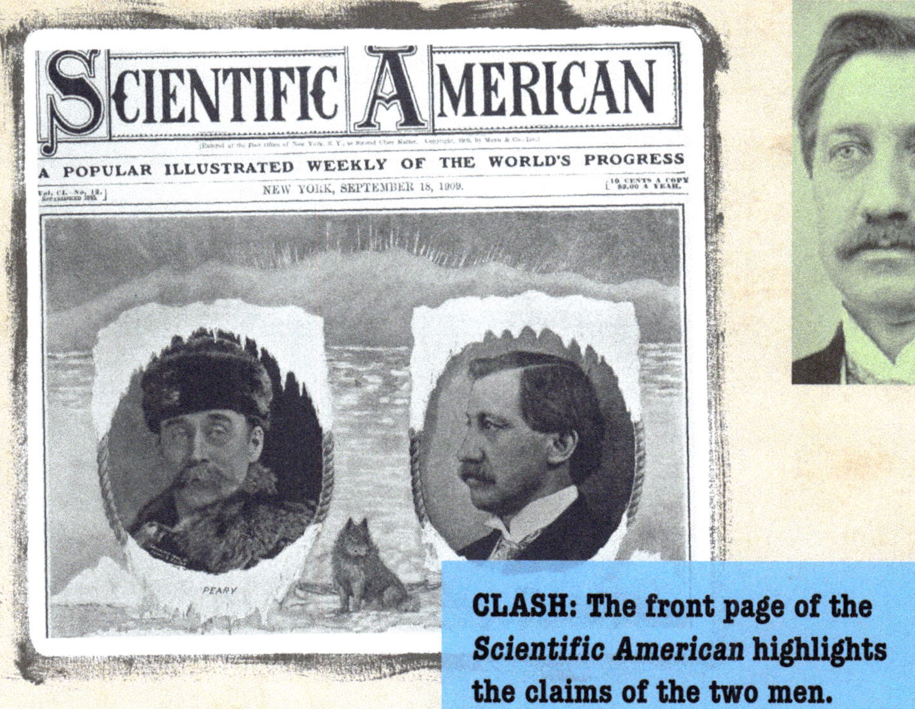

SCIENTIFIC AMERICAN

A POPULAR ILLUSTRATED WEEKLY OF THE WORLD'S PROGRESS

NEW YORK, SEPTEMBER 18, 1909.

CLASH: The front page of the *Scientific American* highlights the claims of the two men.

Two Telegrams

Peary learned that Cook had sent a telegram to the International Bureau for Polar Research on September 1, 1909. In it, Cook claimed that he had reached the North Pole on April 21, 1908. Peary was furious. On September 6, 1909, he sent his own telegram to the *New York Times* claiming that he had reached the North Pole on April 6, 1909. The next day, he sent another telegram discrediting Cook's claim and telling the newspaper that the other explorer's account was dubious and should not be taken seriously.

> **"Cook's story should not be taken too seriously. The two Eskimos who accompanied him say he went no distance north."**

Robert Peary, telegram from Labrador to the *New York Times*, September 7, 1909

PEARY'S CAMPAIGN

FLASH POINT » GATHERING SUPPORT

Early in the fall of 1909, Peary's campaign to discredit Cook's claims to have reached the North Pole became more serious.

In 1898 Peary had founded the Peary Arctic Club to fund his explorations. The club's members were all personal friends of his. In October 1909 the Club said that it had evidence that Cook had been untruthful in the past about his achievements as an explorer.

Cook had made two expeditions to America's highest mountain, Mount McKinley in Alaska, in 1903 and 1906. In 1906 he claimed to have reached the summit with a blacksmith from Montana, Ed Barrill. In the past, Barrill had talked often about the climb. However, in 1909 he swore an affidavit to say that he and Cook had never reached the summit. Many people believed Barrill had been bribed by the Peary

DINNER: The National Geographic Society holds a dinner in Peary's honor.

FOUNDERS: The National Geographic Society was formed in 1888 by a group of explorers and scientists.

Arctic Club to change his story, but the damage was done. If Cook had lied about Mount McKinley, had he told the truth about the trek to the North Pole?

More Doubt

In November a subcommittee of the National Geographic Society examined Peary's claim to have reached the North Pole. The members all knew Peary. They interviewed him but did not ask to see any evidence. Then they announced their belief that Peary had indeed reached the Pole.

> "The subcommittee are unanimously of the opinion that Commander Peary reached the North Pole on April 6, 1909."

Statement from the National Geographic Society, November 4, 1909

COOK'S ABSENCE

FLASH POINT **» THE PRESSURE BEGINS TO BUILD**

Frederick Cook was unable to produce evidence of his own achievement in defense of Peary's claims. He quickly became a national villain.

In September 1909, Cook had embarked on a lecture tour across the country. He planned to give 70 talks about his polar journey in just 24 days. His first lectures were at Carnegie Hall in New York City. They were met with great enthusiasm. Then, however, Peary's campaign to discredit Cook's achievement started to damage his reputation.

PUCK: This magazine cover shows an ice figure weighing the money the two men stand to make from books and lectures.

The public began to doubt Cook's honesty after Ed Barrill's affidavit. Also, Cook's exploration equipment never turned up. Cook was exhausted by constantly having to defend himself. In late October he canceled the rest of his lecture tour and went into hiding.

Worse News Follows

On December 8, 1909, more bad news for Cook came from Denmark. Cook had handed his written records of his expedition to the

FIGHT: This French magazine cartoon from September 1909 pokes fun at the dispute between the two explorers.

> **"For the first time the really worldwide interest in this mad quest began to dawn upon me."**
>
> **Cook quoted in *Hampton's Magazine*, April 1911**

University of Copenhagen. Having examined the documents, Danish experts judged that Cook's discovery of the North Pole was "not proven." Peary's campaign had planted doubt in the minds of the American public. Many people took the verdict of "not proven" to mean Cook's claims were false.

GIVING EVIDENCE

FLASH POINT **» PEARY FACES QUESTIONS**

With Cook in hiding, Peary thought his own claim to have reached the North Pole would now be accepted. He was to be disappointed.

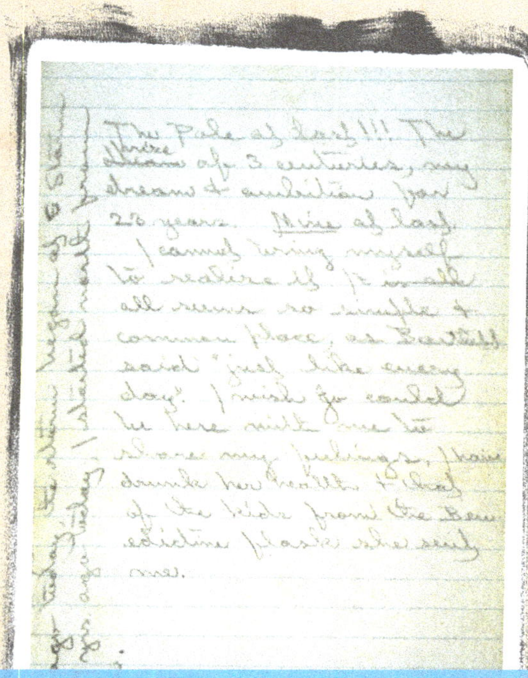

The Pole at last!!! The prize of 3 centuries, my dream & ambition for 23 years. Mine at last. I cannot bring myself to realize it. It all seems so simple & commonplace, as Bartlett said "just like every day". I wish you could be here with me to share my feelings. I have drunk her health & that of the kids from the Benedictine flask she sent me.

JOURNAL: The committee thought the pages of Peary's diary were suspiciously clean for a book carried on a long trip.

Doubts about Peary's own claim to have reached the North Pole had not gone away. There were many concerns about his account of the expedition. Some members of Congress thought it would be best if Peary's account was judged by other explorers. Peary managed to use the influence of the members of the Peary Arctic Club to keep this from happening. Instead, in January 1911 Peary was called to the Naval Affairs Subcommittee to prove that he had reached the North Pole.

A Suspect Diary

As Peary testified in front of the committee, it became clear that the seven committee members had doubts about some of the evidence. Like Frederick Cook, Robert Peary had kept a diary during his expedition. Such personal records were considered important

FAT: Explorers' fingers usually got covered in grease from eating fatty meat called pemmican.

evidence at the time. The members of the committee, however, did not believe the diary looked like a book that had been to the North Pole. The handwriting looked exactly the same for every entry, which made the diary entries look as if they had all been written at the same time. The page for April 6, 1909, the day Peary claimed to have reached the North Pole, was blank. Instead, Peary had inserted a loose-leaf page that included his famous note, "The Pole at Last!" The committee was even more concerned that the diary seemed suspiciously clean. The committee members noted that they would expect it to have greasy fingerprints on the cover and pages. In the

> "It shows no finger marks or rough usage; a very cleanly kept book."

Representative Ernest W. Roberts on Peary's diary, January 1911

> To me, as a member of this committee, I accept your word; but your proofs, I know nothing at all about.

Representative Thomas S. Butler to Peary, January 1911

MEASUREMENT: Peary used a sextant so he could navigate by the stars.

Arctic, explorers ate pemmican, a mixture of ground meat and animal fat that gave them the calories they needed to survive in the bitter cold. Explorers ate pemmican with their fingers, so they left greasy marks everywhere. Peary's diary had no such marks on it.

Inconsistent Details

Another problem with Peary's account was the speed at which he claimed to have traveled. As part of his campaign to discredit Cook, Peary had expressed his doubts about Cook's claim to have covered up to 24 miles (38 km) a day; now Peary himself claimed that he and Henson had covered the last part of their journey doing over 30 miles (48 km) a day. This was despite the fact that, until then, the expedition had been averaging just 12 miles (19 km) a day. In addition, Peary had lost most of his toes to frostbite on an expedition some years earlier, which made walking more difficult for him.

For many years, Peary had claimed that measuring longitude was vital to navigation in the polar region. Longitude measured how far east or west a location was on Earth's surface. During his 1909 attempt on the North Pole, however, Peary measured only his latitude, or how far north he was. Traveling even 100 miles (160 km) without measuring longitude might have resulted in Peary and Henson being up to 50 miles (80 km) east or west of their correct position.

The Committee's Conclusion

In the end, the Naval Affairs Subcommittee voted four to three in favor of awarding Peary the title of rear admiral, along with a rear admiral's pension. But the committee would not confirm that Peary had been the first man to reach the North Pole or give him the title "Discoverer of the North Pole." They merely said Peary had reached it. It was a victory for Peary, but it was also a disappointment.

TIME: Peary carried three chronometers for accurate timekeeping yet failed to use them to help measure his longitude.

COOK'S DISGRACE

» A CRIMINAL CAREER

If Cook thought the controversy surrounding his discovery of the North Pole was the worst thing that could happen, he was to be proved wrong.

After Frederick Cook disappeared from the public eye in 1909 he spent time overseas in South America and Europe. When he returned to the United States, he moved to Texas in 1922. There he became involved in the state's rapidly expanding oil industry. Cook could not escape his past, however, and the old stories of his dishonesty. In 1923, he was accused of exaggerating the value of his oil company in order to mislead investors. The judge at Cook's trial was an old friend of the Peary family. Although 283 witnesses gave evidence about Cook's honesty, he was found guilty and sentenced to nearly 15 years in prison.

FREED: Cook leaves prison in 1930. He was later pardoned by President Franklin D. Roosevelt.

After Jail

Cook was eventually released from Leavenworth Jail,

MARKER: This sign was put up in New Rochelle, New York. It commemorates Cook's family home.

Kansas, in 1930. While Cook was in jail, his friend and supporter Roald Amundsen visited him in 1926. The National Geographic Society, which continued to support Peary and his claims, canceled a planned lecture by Amundsen.

Cook spent the last 10 years of his life out of the public spotlight. In 1940, shortly before his death, President Franklin D. Roosevelt granted him a pardon. Frederick Cook died on August 5, 1940.

> **"I have read Dr. Cook's story and I have read Peary's. In Peary's story I have not found anything of consequence not covered already by Dr. Cook."**

Roald Amundsen, January 24, 1926

A WOUNDED HERO

» DAMAGED REPUTATION

The verdict of the Naval Affairs Subcommittee severely disappointed Peary. He rarely discussed his Arctic expeditions later in his life.

Peary continued to receive much praise for his Arctic exploits. He received 22 honorary medals from different countries and three honorary doctorates. After the committee hearing, however, he was reluctant to discuss his expeditions. The hearing had planted doubt in the public's mind about his achievements. When the committee granted Peary the rank of rear admiral on March 30, 1911 (backdated to April 6, 1909), Peary immediately resigned from the Navy.

WORKING: Peary spent his last years supporting causes he favored.

FUNERAL: Peary was honored by being buried in Arlington National Cemetery in Washington, D.C.

Retirement

Peary retired to Maine. In 1916, he became chairman of the National Aerial Coast Patrol Commission. This organization promoted the use of military and naval aviation to patrol US coasts and led to the formation of Naval Reserve aerial coastal patrol units.

In poor health as the result of his many Arctic expeditions, Peary died on February 20, 1920, at the age of 63.

"Thank God the fight is over! President signed Bill this forenoon."

Telegram from Peary to General T. H. Hubbard, March 4, 1911

AFTERMATH

» REACHING THE NORTH POLE

Doubt about the truth of Robert Peary's claims increased after his death. Frederick Cook's claims were also reexamined.

Explorers traveled to the Arctic throughout the 20th century. They confirmed Cook's descriptions of the polar sea and ice islands, and the westward drift of the polar ice. The first undisputed overland trip to the North Pole was made in 1968, when the Minnesotan Ralph Plaisted reached it by snowmobile.

An Expert Reviews the Evidence

In 1969 the British explorer Wally Herbert made the first undisputed walk to the North Pole. The National Geographic Society asked Herbert to review Peary's notes of his 1909 expedition. Based on his

POLE: Experts now believe Peary did not reach the North Pole, although he came close.

UNDISPUTED: Wally Herbert was the first explorer to definitely reach the North Pole on foot.

own experiences, Herbert concluded that Peary had made up his records and had probably not reached the North Pole. Most people agreed. The National Geographic Society said that Peary probably reached within 5 miles (8 km) of the North Pole.

> "Remember Mother, I must have fame & I cannot reconcile myself to years of commonplace drudgery."
>
> **Robert Peary to his mother, February 27, 1887**

Frederick Cook's papers, which Harry Whitney buried in Greenland, have never been found. However, explorers increasingly believe that Cook probably did reach the North Pole after all.

JUDGMENT

ROBERT PEARY  FREDERICK COOK

From an early age Robert Peary wanted fame at all costs. He also had powerful friends who helped him achieve his goal of worldwide fame.

* Peary was not particularly interested in the Arctic for its own sake. He was more interested in breaking a record.

* Peary often treated the Inuit he met poorly. He brought six Inuit back to the United States as "specimens" for the Museum of Natural History in New York.

* Although Cook had saved Peary when he went missing in 1901, Peary became fiercely critical of his former colleague.

* Peary almost certainly lied to the Naval Affairs Subcommittee and evaded its questions.

Hailed as a hero on his return to the United States, Cook was soon criticized as a liar. Many experts now believe he did reach the North Pole after all.

* **Cook was a kind and thoughtful man who remained modest about his achievements.**

* **Cook was interested in the Inuit and wanted to learn about them as much as he wanted to reach the North Pole.**

* **Cook's claim to have climbed Mount McKinley was never proven. That cast lasting doubt on his honesty.**

* **Cook was jailed for fraud. While he was in jail, Cook was popular with prisoners and staff alike.**

TIMELINE

Robert Peary and Frederick Cook both wanted to reach the North Pole first. Their competing claims led to a very public quarrel that dominated world news throughout 1909 and beyond.

1893

Falling Out
Frederick Cook quits Robert Peary's expedition to Greenland after he refuses to promise that he will not write about the trip before Peary himself.

1906

Disputed Claim
In September, Cook claims to become the first man to reach the top of Mount McKinley in Alaska. His claim is later widely disputed.

1907

Cook Sets Out
In July, Frederick Cook sails from New York to Greenland, where he announces his intention to try to reach the North Pole.

1908

Cook at the Pole
On April 21, Cook claims to reach the North Pole with two Inuit, Etukishook and Ahwelah; their journey back to Greenland takes nearly 14 months.

Peary Sets Out
On July 6, Robert Peary sails from New York for Greenland on board the SS *Roosevelt* in order to try to reach the North Pole.

1909

Peary at the Pole
On April 6, Peary and Matthew Henson claim to reach the North Pole with their Inuit companions.

Cook's Return
On August 21, Frederick Cook receives a hero's welcome on his return to New York; few people doubt his claim to have reached the North Pole.

Two Telegrams
Early in September, both explorers send telegrams claiming to have reached the North Pole first; Peary also states that Cook's claim is false.

Peary's Campaign
In fall, Peary begins a campaign to discredit Cook with backing from his own supporters, including the National Geographic Society.

Cook Under Pressure
In October, the Peary Arctic Club produces a legal statement that Cook's claim to have climbed Mount McKinley in 1906 was fake. Doubts begin to grow about Cook's trustworthiness.

Cook Disappears
In late October, Cook pulls out halfway through a lecture tour of the United States. He travels to Europe and South America and remains out of the media.

1911

Peary's Committee
In January, Peary appears before the Naval Affairs Subcommittee; after a three-day hearing, the committee decides that he had probably but not definitely reached the North Pole.

GLOSSARY

affidavit A written statement that is signed as being true by the writer in the presence of a legal official.

airship A large aircraft with a body made from a balloon inflated with gas.

archipelago A large body of water with many islands.

cache To put objects in a hiding place, especially in the ground.

chronometer A highly accurate clock used for navigation.

crevasse A deep, narrow split in the ice of a glacier.

discredit To try to show that something is untrue or untrustworthy.

dog sled A sled with skis that is pulled by dogs.

frostbite Damage to the skin and flesh caused by long exposure to cold temperatures; frostbite often affects the fingers, toes, or nose.

honor An award given in recognition of an achievement.

indigenous Describes something that originates in a particular place.

introspective Describes someone quiet and thoughtful.

Inuit A people who live inside the Arctic Circle in North America and Greenland.

investors People who use their money to fund businesses in return for future profits.

latitude The measure of someone's position north or south of an imaginary line drawn around Earth.

longitude The measure of someone's position east or west of an imaginary line drawn around Earth.

pack ice Pieces of floating ice that are driven together by wind or currents to form a single sheet of ice.

pemmican Cakes of food made from dried, powdered meat mixed with fat and sometimes dried fruit or berries.

philanthropist A wealthy person who uses his or her money to help other people.

polar Related to the North or South Pole.

relay The act of passing something along from one person to another; also, a race that is divided into sections.

reputation How someone is thought of or regarded by others.

sextant A device used to measure the position of the sun, planets, or stars above the horizon for use in navigation.

smirched Made dirty or stained.

telegram A message sent by telegraph, which uses electronic signals and wires to communicate over long distances.

whaler A ship used for hunting and catching whales.

FOR FURTHER INFORMATION

Books

Anderson, Harry S. *Exploring the Polar Regions* (Discovery & Exploration). Chelsea House Publishing, 2009.

Bedesky, Baron. *Peary and Henson: The Race to the North Pole* (In the Footsteps of Explorers). Crabtree Publishing Company, 2006.

Dunn, Joeming W., and Ben Dunn. *Reaching the North Pole* (Graphic History). Looking Glass Library, 2008.

Hoena, Blake A., and Phil Miller. *Matthew Henson: Arctic Adventurer* (Graphic Biographies). Capstone Press, 2005.

Petrie, Kristin. *Robert Peary* (Explorers). Checkerboard Library, 2007.

Websites

www.pbs.org/wgbh/amex/ice/index.html
Site to support the PBS documentary about Peary, *Alone on the Ice*, with special features and timeline.

www.frederickcooksociety.org
The website of the Frederick A. Cook Society, with links to many articles about the controversy.

humbug.polarhist.com
A site by polar scholar Robert M. Bryce entitled "Frederick A. Cook: from Hero to Humbug."

www.eyewitnesstohistory.com/vopeary.htm
Peary's own description of reaching the North Pole, from Eyewitness to History.

gardenofpraise.com/ibdpeary.htm
A biography of Robert Peary from Garden of Praise.

polardiscovery.whoi.edu/arctic/timeline.html
Timeline of the exploration of the Arctic.

INDEX